Do-It-Yourself Private Investigations:
Online Dating, Suspected Infidelity, Missing Persons and more

Darren Lee

DISCLAIMER

The material in this publication is of a general nature, and neither purports nor intends to be advice. This publication is sold with the understanding that neither the author, nor publisher is engaged in rendering legal, or other professional service. If legal advice or other expert assistance is required, the services of a competent professional person in your legal jurisdiction should be sought. The author and publisher expressly disclaim all and any liability to any person, whether a purchaser of this publication or not, in respect of anything and of the consequences done or omitted to be done by any such person in reliance, whether whole or partial, upon the whole or any part of the contents of this publication.

DEDICATION

There is little in this world more suppressive than the uncertainty of mystery. This book is dedicated to those with the courage to take the action necessary to obtain the information they need to make decisions and not have the wool pulled over their eyes by those who desire their ignorance.

The skills you will learn in this text will change you. Please use them responsibly.

Do-It-Yourself Private Investigations

Do-It-Yourself Private Investigations

CONTENTS

ACKNOWLEDGMENTS

Acknowledgment must be made to the old school private investigator, forced to dive through trash bins in the middle of the night and resort to other unsavory methods to get the data they needed. The modern age of investigations has certainly been much simpler for those of my generation for which I am grateful.

I would also like to thank my family and friends who listened to my countless hours of updating them on new techniques I had identified which were for the large part outside of their area of interest and reality. They always said I should put this in a book some day and that time has come.

Do-It-Yourself Private Investigations

PREFACE

Few delve into the world of private investigations and do not change as human beings. The skills you will learn in this brief volume will change you. They are used daily by law enforcement, intelligence agencies, recruitment agencies, as well as insurance companies and their lawyers/private investigators and yet very little has been published to the general public on this area. It is my intention to break that silence. As the old saying goes, 'Knowledge is Power', and if you want to succeed in life, the value in having the ability to correctly estimate people and situations cannot be underestimated. However, with knowledge comes responsibility, and it is my sincere hope that you use these techniques morally and not to bring unjust pain and confusion to the lives of others.

I have worked as both a private investigator and insurance defence lawyer for many years. In addition to that I have an extensive background in online reputation management and uncovering the true identities of those behind internet based attacks, defamation and bullying.

The idea of this text is therefore to train you on how modern private investigations are performed so that you are i) equipped to conduct your own private investigations; and ii) better informed on the role a private investigator may play in your investigation, should you choose to hire one.

Although the resources in each country vary considerably due to the different degrees of strictness in Freedom of Information and other privacy laws, the techniques found in this text are intended to be applicable to an international audience.

The skills you will learn here are applicable to all manner of investigations such as infidelity, corporate espionage, missing persons, wills, family disputes and child abuse.

Yours Sincerely

Darren Lee

Do-It-Yourself Private Investigations

1 INVESTIGATION PLAN

At the outset of any investigation ask yourself:

i)   What data do you have?
ii)   What data do you want?
iii) What are your resources?
iv)   What is your budget for this investigation in terms of time, effort and finances?

A do-it-yourself investigation would generally go through **5 phases** depending on the level of complexity of the investigation:

i)   Gathering known information;

ii)   Gathering publicly available information. This is termed Open Source Intelligence or OSINT;

iii) Approaching human resources. This is termed Human Intelligence, or HUMINT;

iv)   Paying for advanced database searches; and

v)   Hiring a professional investigator.

The following are scenarios in which you would gather known information, and the remaining 5 phases are covered in the remainder of this text.

Infidelity

With infidelity, cases you should go with your instincts and if you believe your partner is cheating, they probably are.

However, if you require harder evidence on them, you must clear your mind of any preconceived ideas you have about the situation and approach your investigation in an objective and detached fashion to reduce the risk of you *seeing what you want to see*.

If you suspect your partner is cheating on you, you should build a profile on them based on their ordinary habit patterns. You should then monitor them for activities which deviate from these ordinary habit patterns which collectively may provide clues of infidelity. Such monitoring should include:

- Maintaining a written journal of their departure/arrival times each day from home.
- Monitoring their records and photograph them where possible – phone bills, receipts, bank withdrawals, diary entries.
- Checking their car odometer to see what distance they are covering each day.
- Checking for indications they have showered before returning home.
- Observing whether they are washing their clothes more often than normal.
- Looking of inconsistencies in stories about their day.
- Monitoring any suspicious friends who have been newly added to their Facebook friends list.
- Monitor the call log on their phone (if you can access it) or on their phone bill.

Do not confront your partner yet, but instead give them an opportunity to tell you various stories about their daily activities, which you can then confront them on once you have a tighter evidence of inconsistencies.

Missing Person

If you are concerned about a person you believe has gone missing, first ask yourself whether they could be intentionally hiding and why that may be. Then build a profile on them by considering:

- Where they were last seen?
- Who are their known friends and associates?
- Look for clues on their Facebook profile as to places they intended to go.
- Where do their relatives live?
- Are they responding to phone calls?
- What is their sexual preference?
- Do they belong to any clubs?
- What work do they perform?
- Do they have any regular appointments?

Do-It-Yourself Private Investigations

2 DESKTOP INVESTIGATIONS

After collecting all known information on a person, the next stage of building a profile on somebody, will be to use publicly available resources such as the internet and social media to collect information on them. In the private investigations world, this is loosely termed a <u>desktop investigation</u> as the majority of it can be done with phone calls and the internet - although some travel may be necessary. Data which will assist at this stage includes their:

- Current or former email address
- Mobile phone number
- Landline phone number
- Former addresses
- Photographs
- Social media profile photos
- Vehicle details
- Known friends/associates
- Recreation clubs/bars/childcare centres or other places the person of interest may frequent
- Sports or hobbies
- Spouse or other family members' work places/schools

Before we dive into the technical resources used in desktop investigations consider the following scenario:

> *You suspect your partner of infidelity. You overhear him late at night speaking in a hushed tone with somebody on the phone and as he says goodbye he calls the other person on the phone, "Kate", and later calls her "blondie". When*

you walk passed him he nervously tells you that he thought you were asleep and quickly walks up to you and gives you a hug. You are concerned that you do not yet have sufficient evidence to confront him about cheating on you as you don't want him to cover his tracks at this early stage. You go onto his Facebook profile and find two attractive women named Kate on his Facebook friends list. One of the women has red hair and the other is wearing a hat so you cannot tell her hair colour. You google search this woman's name and find a Linkedin profile photo of somebody who looks like her but now revealing her hair to be blonde. You perform an electoral role name check and find a matching address for the blonde Kate. Looking through the records you have retained of your partner's vehicle odometer readings, you have noticed that on Wednesdays and Fridays he has been travelling 10km more per day than on the other days indicating he is not only attending his office where he works as an accountant but also attending somewhere else. He has been giving you the excuse on these days that he has been staying back late at work for 2 hours to catch up on files. At this stage you could hire two licensed private investigators to monitor both Kate's house and follow your partner from work. By hiring two investigators you will considerably increase the chance of recording any time these two may be spending together as if one investigator loses your partner at a traffic light, the other investigator will continue to trail Kate and eventually the two may meet up.

When conducting a desktop investigation, keep records of each piece of data you identify with exact details on whether it has been confirmed as a positive lead or a possible lead. For example:

i)   If you find a Facebook profile for somebody which matches their mobile phone number, that could be considered a **positive lead**; and

ii) However, if you only find a Facebook profile for somebody which matches their name and you are not yet sure if this is the person you are looking for, that would be a **possible lead** requiring further confirmation.

Using data from the profile you have pieced together so far, commence your desktop investigation. Each time a new clue is found, utilise that in your searches.

Scenario

> *You are conducting a search on a mobile number you found written on a note in your business partner's desk which you believe may belong to somebody they wish to go into business with in competition with you. You google search this mobile number and identify an advertisement on gumtree.com.au for a car for sale. You email the contact person listed on this advertisement posing as an interested purchaser. The person emails you back revealing their name as 'John', the email address as 'john889@hotmail.com' and their address as '67 Bell Street, Midland'. You can now use each of these 3 pieces of new information to add to your desktop investigation. For example, by google searching the address and checking for a Facebook profile connected with the email address.*

Resources

- *Search engines*

Popular search engines such as google.com and yahoo.com should be used as a starting point for a desktop investigation. Use the localised version of the search engine for your country such as google.com.au and yahoo.com.au for Australia.

We will assume that you have at least a basic understanding of how search engines operate but here are some search operators from google.com to help make your search process more specific:

site:	Get results from certain sites or domains. Examples: Olympics site:nbc.com and Olympics site: .gov
link:	Find pages that link to a certain page. Example: link:youtube.com
related:	Find sites that are similar to a web address you already know. Example: related:time.com
OR	Find pages that might use one of several words. Example: marathon OR race
info:	Get information about a web address, including the cached version of the page, similar pages, and pages that link to the site. Example: info:google.com
cache:	See what a page looks like the last time Google visited the site. Example: cache:washington.edu
-	When you use a dash before a word or site, it excludes sites with that info from your results. This is useful for words with multiple meanings, like Jaguar the car brand and jaguar the animal. Examples: jaguar speed -car or pandas -site:wikipedia.org
"	When you put a word or phrase in quotes, the

	results will only include pages with the same words in the same order as the ones inside the quotes. Only use this if you're looking for an exact word or phrase, otherwise you'll exclude many helpful results by mistake. Example: "imagine all the people"
*	Add an asterisk as a placeholder for any unknown or wildcard terms. . Example: "a * saved is a * earned"

- *Facebook.com*

Facebook is arguably the most popular social network in the world and its value in profiling cannot be underestimated. From Facebook, you can very quickly get an idea of what somebody looks like, who their friends are, where they work, what they do for fun, where they live and who their family members are – all of which are invaluable to private investigations.

There are a few ways to use Facebook.

Obviously, if you are friends with the person of interest on Facebook, then you have a considerable advantage as (depending on their privacy settings) you will have unrestricted access to their friends list, posts, photos, videos, events they are attending, etc. If you can befriend the person of interest on Facebook it is highly recommended you do so to gain this greater depth of insight into their profile, unless to do so would place your identity or personal information at risk.

Dependent on their privacy settings, a person of interest may only allow limited access to their profile from members of the public with whom they have not added as friends. However, you can often still see limited posts on their wall and at a minimum their profile photo.

Facebook has an advanced search function whereby you can search for specific variables such as everybody who attended a particular school, which females attended a particular school, people of a particular name and living in a particular location, etc as well as comparing the interests of two Facebook users.

The easiest way to use this functions at the following website with Mozilla firefox, while you are logged into Facebook:

https://inteltechniques.com/OSINT/Facebook.html

Scenario

> You are trying to locate an old friend you went to high school with. You cannot remember her last name but know her name is Kim, she went to Sorone Senior High School and is currently living in Sydney. Your search term on Facebook would be a variation of: "People named Kim who went to Sorone Senior High School and live in Sydney."

Using Facebook's search function for profiles matching email addresses and phone numbers can be hit and miss depending on the privacy settings set by the person you are trying to locate. A simple way to check whether a Facebook profile is connected to an email address or a mobile phone number is to search it using Facebook's *lost password recovery function* at https://www.Facebook.com/login/identify.

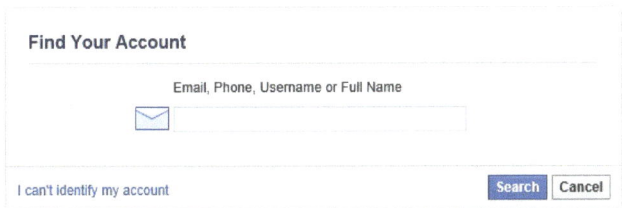

This will rapidly tell you whether the person has a Facebook profile so you can:

i) Verify that the phone number/email address is valid; and

ii) Possibly identify the name or profile photo connected with the profile which although you cannot click on it directly from the forgot password results to view their profile, if you return to Facebook's ordinary search bar and type in the now identified person's name, you can scroll down to find which profile matches the profile photo you have now seen.

*** Once you get the result from typing in the email address or phone number above, do not click further than this screen as it may alert the person of interest that you are attempting to reset their password. However, if you do not click further than this screen, they will not find out about it.

- *People Search Engines*

In addition to searching general search engines such as google for somebodies name (and geographical area or other data to narrow down the result), the following websites can also be used:

11

- o Pipl.com
- o Peepdb.com
- o http://thatsthem.com/name-address-search
- o http://www.reversegenie.com/people.php
- o Zoominfo.com
- o Intelius.com

Additionally, to search these and several other people search websites all at the same time to maximise the efficiency of the search and increase the likelihood of a positive match, you could use the following site (which must be used with Mozilla Firefox): https://inteltechniques.com/OSINT/person.html

The matches for each of these sites vary and will generally identify more on American persons of interest based on their relaxed freedom of information laws.

- • *Reverse Image Search*

If you identify a photograph of somebody on the internet, there is a method which can be used to find out where else on the internet that photo appears. NOTE: the results are most effective for this search method when using a photo which already appears on the internet such as a Facebook profile photo, as opposed to a newly taken photograph.

This function is provided at google.com/images by clicking on the camera icon in the diagram below and uploading the photo.

Search by image   ×

Search Google with an image instead of text. Try dragging an image here.

Paste image URL   Upload an image 🖼

Browse… No file selected.

Scenario

You suspect your partner of infidelity. You reverse image search his Facebook profile photo and identify that photo has also been used as his profile photo for a dating website.

Scenario

You own a phone sales company. You realize you are being undercut by a seller on ebay who is selling the same phones you are selling for ½ the price. You reverse image search each of the phone images on the ebay website and identify the exact same images are being used to sell phones from a Chinese store. This may provide a lead that the ebay seller is obtaining the phones from the Chinese store. Further

research could be performed on the Chinese store to identify a way to reduce their dealings with the ebay seller.

Scenario

You meet a man whom you believe is the love of your life on a dating website. He sends you a photo of himself and describes himself as being from Spain and having never been out of his country before. You reverse search this photo and find it matches a photo of an amateur model in Russia.

Advanced Tip: There are several extensions for the internet browsers, Mozilla Firefox and Chrome, which will speed up the reverse image process by allowing you to right click on an image and select the option in the pop up menu to reverse image search the picture (eg. The Google Reverse Image Extension):

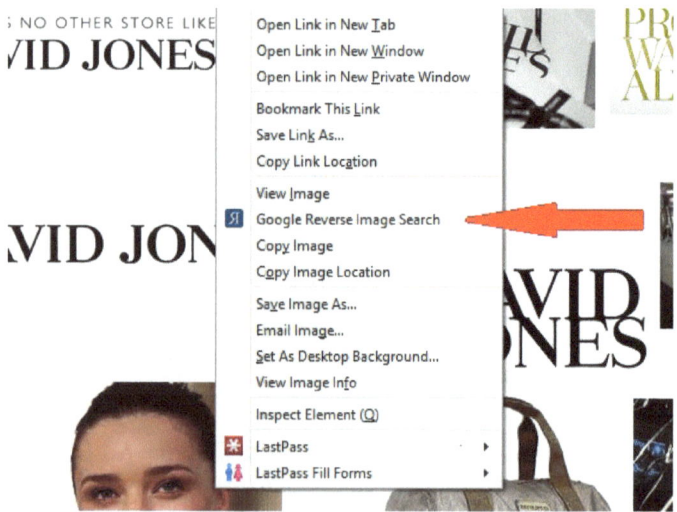

- *Username*

People often use alternative names on social media/blogging websites, termed pen names, handles, monikers, aliases, etc. For example, John Smith's username on youtube.com may be Johnno989.

People are creatures of habit and will often use the same username for their accounts on multiple websites. Additionally, the username may provide a clue to their email address, such as johnno989@hotmail.com for the above example.

It is therefore useful to perform at least a search engine search on this username to see what else can be dug up. Additional sites on which usernames can be searched for matching social media profiles include:

o pipl.com/username
o knowem.com
o usernamecheck.com
o namechk.com
o namevine.com
o usersearch.org
o usersherlock.com
o thatsthem.com/social-id-search

The results from each of these websites varies dependent on geographical location and other factors such as the social media sites being searched by each of these resources.

Scenario

> *You receive a threatening email from the email address stalker8988@hotmail.com telling you to shut down your Australian based furniture store. You perform a google search engine search of this email address to see who it may be connected with and do not identify any positive results. You search the username stalker8988 on pipl.com/username and identify the youtube channel youtube.com/stalker8988. This youtube channel includes subscriptions to several furniture store youtube channels including your company's own youtube channel! This provides a strong lead that the stalker8988@hotmail.com youtube channel is connected to the sender of the threatening email. In the 'about' section of the stalker8988 youtube channel is listed a contact number of 0428 995 665. You then check this phone number using Facebook's lost*

password recovery function (as discussed under the Facebook section above) and identify a Facebook profile for 'John Smith' a known competitor to your business.

The following link will enable you to search several of the main dating websites for matches to that username: https://inteltechniques.com/osint/dating.networks.html

- Email addresses

There is no reliable database in which you can search somebodies name or mobile number and obtain their email address. For this reason, you need to be more creative.

Using the lost password recovery function of Facebook (described in the above Facebook section), you could type in the person of interest's mobile number or name and the next screen may provide you with a clue as what the email address may be. You should see a screen like this:

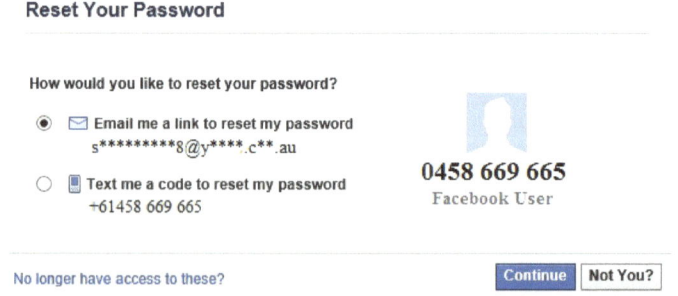

Note that the email address is blanked out. The last part is likely to be yahoo.com.au. However, this could be used to guess the person's email address based on what you know about the person. This could be:

- A username they use on social media. Eg. They are called stalker8988 on their youtube channel. Therefore the email address may be stalker8988@yahoo.com.au
- A mixture of the first initial of the name with the last name;
- There first name with their last name's initial.

Once you think you have a match, type that email address back into Facebook's password recovery section. You will see a screen like this:

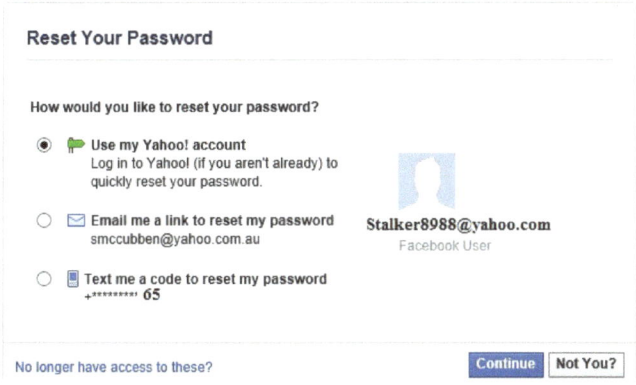

Note that this email address matches a phone number which ends in 65. This provides a highly likely match between the guessed email address of stalker8988@yahoo.com and the mobile number 0458 669 665.

Once you have an email address for somebody, search it using a search engine to see what comes up (possible business listing, second hand goods sales advertisements such as craigslist, gumtree, etc). The following websites should also be searched to see which social media accounts the email address is connected to or websites the person of interest could be hosting:

- o Pipl.com
- o Reversegenie.com/email.php
- o http://thatsthem.com/find-people-email-search
- o Emailsherlock.com
- o https://whoisology.com/#advanced

Scenario

> *You run an art gallery. You are contacted from the email address leonardo@indonesiaart.com by a man named Leonardo claiming to be a multi-millionaire art dealer asking you to fly to Indonesia to meet him and discuss selling your art. You want to do some research on Leonardo before you meet him. This email address is a starting point for your research. You search the email address on pipl.com and discover a Facebook profile listing Leonordo as living in Spain. You also go to Indonesiaart.com and discover the website is tacky and amateurish. Suspicious of Leonardo, you make small talk with him by email and ask him for a phone number you can contact him on. You then google search his phone number and find it is listed on a website warning you that he is a scammer from Spain who preys on unsuspecting victims and does not even live in Indonesia.*

- • *Phone numbers*

When you receive a phone number for somebody you should immediately perform searches on it to see what the number is connected to.

Which databases you use will depend on what country the phone number is connected to. The following are some of the popular phone number search websites:

https://www.Facebook.com/login/identify?ctx=	Facebook's password recovery function as discussed above

recover	under the heading 'Facebook'
http://thatsthem.com/reverse-phone-search	Useful for American phone numbers
Whocalld.com	Useful for American phone numbers
Reversegenie.com	Useful for American phone numbers
Reverseaustralia.com.au	Useful for Australian phone numbers
Slydial.com	This will call an American phone number and go straight through to the voicemail greeting without alerting the person of interest
Truecaller.com	This site is growing in popularity. Users of an android app agree to anonymously share their phone book with other users of the app in exchange for being able to view names of people phoning them which are listed in Truecaller's user created database. Therefore, you can reverse search a phone number to identify what names other people have saved that number in their phone as. Eg.

	0452998995 may be saved as Blonde Hooker which could give you a hint that the person of interest may be working as a prostitute. Useful to search international numbers.

Standard phone directories such as the yellow and whites pages in each country should also be searched for person and business names in an attempt to identify phone numbers.

Scenario

> *You have noticed your husband has been spending more and more late nights at the office, there has been a strong perfume smell in his car over the last few weeks and his sexual appetite has decreased significantly. You believe he may be seeing prostitutes. You check his phone and see there was an entry for the number 0458 665 995 being called at midnight on Friday night. You check this number on truecaller.com and find it is listed as Blondie Big Red's Angels. You search the term 'Big Red's Angels' and find it is a brothel.*

- Domain name

If you identify a website domain name the following searches can be performed on it.

Search the site on http://www.domainhistory.net. This will give you a historical listing of the registrant details for that site including, the contact details of the registrant. There are many other similar websites, but this one will give the history of the registrant details which can be useful in case the current registrant details are concealed through a service like Domains By Proxy - paid service in which domain registrant reports conceal the website registrant's contact and contact details by displaying entries such as:

Whois Lookup Date: 08-29-14

Domain Name: HOWTOBEABOUNCER.NET

Registrar URL: http://www.godaddy.com

Registrant Name: Registration Private

Registrant Organization: Domains By Proxy, LLC

Name Server: NS53.DOMAINCONTROL.COM

Name Server: NS54.DOMAINCONTROL.COM

DNSSEC: unsigned

- *Additional Resources*

Inteltechniques.com/links	This website is hosted by world renowned OSINT expert, Michael Bazzell, and provides advanced search tools which you should become familiar with. It is freely accessible and although some of the resources are specific to America, much of it is also publicly accessible. For example, with a username, the tools on this website will automatically search through multiple sites which specialise in locating social media profiles and email addresses connected to usernames; they will also search multiple search engines at the same time; perform advanced Facebook searches, and many more advanced

	functions. The resources on this website are tested and updated weekly as the resources constantly evolve. For this reason, the author has not gone into detail on these resources, but strongly encourage you to become familiar with them. Custom Search Tools Training Guides Search Engines Facebook Google Plus Twitter Smaller Networks Maps Photos Archives
Echosec.net	This site will search geographical locations for social media posts. For example, you are searching for Bill Jones whom you know used to live at 89 Jones Street, Northbridge 10 years ago. You perform an Echosec search over this address and identify a child's flickr.com social media account under the name, Sam Jones. This could provide a possible lead that Bill Jones is still residing at that

	address, although additional confirmatory information would still be required.
Changedetect ion.com	This site will monitor changes on a website/social media account and immediately email you when they occur. For example, this could be used to monitor a business competitor's website or Linkedin profile for changes.
https://maps .google.com and instantstreetv iew.com	These websites will allow you to view a geographical location and get images of that area (usually a few years old). If you are, for example, looking to purchase a property located in a particular area you could use these resources as part of your due diligence to get a quick idea of the surrounding area. It is also invaluable for picking up clues such as the business name written on a sign at an address or what type of car is in the driveway at a house.
Archive.org	This site will display archived versions of websites going back many years. For example, you find a business website of a newly emerging competitor and are

	wondering who was involved in establishing this business. You could view an archived version of the website to see if it displays any staff names/photos.
Torguard.net	The subscription software from this website will allow you to change the IP address of your computer to that of most countries in the world. It is referred to as a VPN (Virtual Private Network) and is useful when conducting desktop investigations to access resources available in other countries which are not ordinarily accessible in your country. It also reduces the risk of leaving your digital footprints behind, which depending on the security level of your investigation, may be important.
Electoral role	Depending on what country you are in, electoral roles are ordinarily available to be searched by the public. In Australia electoral roles can be searched at the Australian Electoral Commission offices in each electoral district and provide addresses for Australian Citizens who are eligible to vote.
Freedom of Information	Freedom of information laws vary between countries. By way of example, America has considerably more relaxed freedom of information laws than Australia. However, the general rule is that

	information held by the government can be obtained by a freedom of information request subject to exceptions such as not revealing personal data (other than your own), security protections, and commercial sensitivity. There is generally an application fee plus cost of photocopying and manpower to fulfil the freedom of information request.

3 PEOPLE

Once you have exhausted your publicly available resources, you will be ready to move to the next stage of developing leads from people either in person or by another means such as telephone or email.

During the course of any investigation, it is inevitable that you will need to extract information from people or steer them in such a direction which will assist your investigation. Much has been written on this area, which is known in the law enforcement/private investigations world as HUMINT (Human Intelligence). Computer hackers call this form of intelligence, 'social engineering', and is essentially aligning yourself with what motivates a person to bring them into alignment with your objectives.

Think of a time when you went for a job interview. Did you tailor your resume to fit the job? How did you dress? What did you say? What were mannerisms like? Did you research the company and likes/dislikes of the managing director beforehand? Why did you do these things? Would you act/dress the same at a job interview for McDonalds as you would for a job as a real estate agent?

Like attending a job interview, the art of persuading people during the course of your investigation requires that you research what the other person is going to expect you to be like and matching that. This takes time and research to master and is an area which can be supplemented by a thorough desktop investigation and generally finding out what you can from other people and resources at your disposal.

To influence anybody it is first necessary to be truly in communication with them. Think of a time when a salesman was trying to sell you something which you were not interested in and they just kept persisting in trying to sell it to you. Chances are you just politely excused yourself, kept walking away and they did not get the sale. This is because you were not truly in communication with each other. To be in communication, it is necessary to match the other person as best you can so they can relate to you.

For example, suppose your person of interest is a troubled teenage male. Chances are he will open up to you more if you speak in the same sort of slang terminology he does, imitate his slouching posture, speak with the same sort of slur and communication lag he does, etc as opposed to approaching him as an authoritative parental figure.

Keep an eye out for the people surrounding your person of interest who are in a better position to obtain the information you need from the person of interest than yourself. These people may be able to be influenced (knowingly or unknowingly) to assist you and thereby keep you at a distance from the person of interest.

Scenario:

> *You own a law firm and are considering promoting your litigation senior associate, David, to partnership but need to test his loyalties before investing further resources into him. You ask your friend, who owns a rival law firm, to approach a recruitment company looking for a senior associate in litigation for a new role. The recruiter (with some gentle encouragement) is likely to then approach David and ask him what salary he would be looking for to leave his current job. This data would be relayed by the recruiter back to your friend who would pass it on to you without you directly approaching David on the issue.*

In the above scenario, David's guard was down while he was speaking with a recruiter. Wherever you detect your person of interest has any kind of a guard up or there is some barrier to you getting them to originate the information you need, it is necessary to disarm those obstacles.

A classic example, is a man, John, trying to get an attractive female, Sally's, phone number at a bar. Sally is likely to have her guard up because a bar is a normal place where men are likely to approach her. Additional barriers could include Sally's desire to retain a good reputation in front of her friends and a fear of being sexually assaulted by a stranger. These barriers make an indirect approach by John to Sally more likely to get her phone number. One such approach may be for John to encourage a female friend of his to make friends with Sally's friends. Sally's friends then encourage John to join their group and he could be introduced to Sally that way. Sally's guard is likely to now be lowered as she can see that John has another female friend (social validation) and John was invited to join their group by Sally's friends and hence must have been approved of by them.

Always present yourself in a manner which is most likely to get the information you need from the person of interest. This is very much a task of acting in which you literally become the person you wish to portray. This should be embodied in your mannerisms, your clothes, how you talk, how you walk - no detail is too small. Most importantly is that each of these factors be congruent with each other so you appear genuine to the person of interest.

When you misrepresent certain aspects of your identity to obtain information, it is referred to as a 'pretext'. Although each country is different, it is generally not illegal to pretend to be somebody you are not unless you are pretending to be a real person or public authority such as a police officer.

When conducting a pretext phone call, it is important to plan it out beforehand so you are prepared no matter which direction the call goes. It is a good idea to appear to be providing information yourself during this call to the person you are speaking with so they feel encouraged to reciprocate. For example, you telling them your name will encourage them to tell you their name. Females are often best for pretext calls as they help to lower the guard of the person being called, although this is just a general observation and of course it depends on the nature of the enquiries.

Willingness and authority to provide information

In any situation where you need to extract information from another person, it is important to ask yourself what leverage you have. Look beyond the fact that you are nice person in need of assistance and go for something stronger: *Appeal to the person's self-interest and willingness to talk to you.*

Scenario

> *You are worried about where your son is one night. He is known to take drugs and you are scared as he has not been home for 48 hours. You notice that his last Facebook update said he was with his friend Sam doing fishing. You do not want to directly tell Sam that you are worried about your son in case Sam lies about your son's whereabouts in an attempt to either protect your son or you from knowing the truth about where he is and what he is doing that night. You instead, phone Sam's mother, who tells you that Sam has also been missing for 48 hours and is not answering his phone when Sam's mother calls. She tells you that the last*

she knew Sam was going to a party at the Duxton Hotel in the city. You are hesitant to phone the Duxton Hotel, as you do not know whose name the hotel room is booked under.

You attend the Duxton Hotel in person, show the front receptionist a photo of your son and ask if she has seen him. She says she hasn't, apologises and you are left having failed to gather a confirmed room of where your son may be.

A better approach would have been to walk up to the counter with urgency, ask the receptionist if you can speak to the manager about an emergency situation. Tell the manager that you have reason to believe your son may be seriously ill or dead at the hotel and you need to locate him asap. Give the manager a copy of his photograph and ask him to show it to his staff asap and check the CCTV footage for the approximate time her son may have entered the hotel. The manager will be more prepared to assist in an emergency situation because of course he does not want a dead body, or seriously ill person to be found at his hotel where he and the hotel could be held at least partially responsible. This is a better approach, than merely asking the receptionist who is not in a position to pass around the photograph of your son to all staff, and also would not be as concerned about legal liability as the manager would be.

Resources

The following resources can be useful in phone pretexts by allowing you to change your caller id when phoning or texting a number and can be used internationally:

Spoofcard.com	This site (also available as a smartphone app) will allow you to phone somebody and change the caller id you phone

	displays as to be any number you choose. For example, if your child is refusing to answer your phone calls, you could call them and have your called id display on their phone as their best friend, Tom, and hence encourage them to answer the phone. However, of course this function should be used with caution for legal reasons.
SpoofText 	This is a smartphone app which allows you to send an SMS text message to somebody and have the sender caller id appear on the person of interest's phone as whatever number you choose.

Scenario

You are trying to get somebodies address and only have their mobile number. You want your caller id to appear as an official looking number to encourage the person to answer your phone call. Using the spoofcard app on your phone, you change your caller id to the number 9400 2000 and phone the person of interest. You claim to be a courier for a general sounding courier service such as Parcel Direct Couriers and tell the person you have a parcel for them but the label on the package is blurred out from rain damage and ask for their home address and time they will be home. If they ask what the package is, base your answer on the research you have done on the person so far. Eg. If it is a 21 year old female whose Facebook profile indicates she likes beauty products, tell her it is a small pearl white box from an American address to encourage her to tell you her address.

Do-It-Yourself Private Investigations

4 GADGETS

There are a wide variety of gadgets which can be used to aid your investigation. However, the legality of their use is highly questionable depending on the circumstances. For example, whereas it may be lawful to install a hidden camera or GPS tracking device in your own vehicle which may be used by your person of interest, it would not be to install a hidden camera in, for example, your work partner's office.

Although I do not profess to educate you on the legality of these devices, it is important that you are at least be aware of them, if for no other reason than it enhances your knowledge of methods which could be used to spy on you. If you are conducting an investigation on somebody else, what is to say they are not watching you too?

The following is a key list of gadgets, many of which can be obtained from ebay or your local friendly spy store:

USB Key Logger	This device is attached in-between a computer's keyboard and the PC/Mac computer. It will record everything typed on the keyboard and hence could be used to obtain passwords, phone numbers and other sensitive data. Average cost - $120AU

Spy Clock	This device will commence recording video and sound when it detects motion. Average cost - $40AU
Spy Pen	This device operates as a real pen with ink, but has a hidden camera and microphone inside. Average cost - $29AU

Spy keyring	Although this device looks like a car immobiliser on the exterior, it has a hidden camera and microphone inside. Average cost - $25AU 
GPS Tracker	This device is around the same size as a wallet. It can be concealed in a vehicle and using mobile networks and GPS technology will transmit its address location which can be viewed via the internet on a website such as that shown below. This device is accurate within 4 metres and its battery lasts for around 6 days, which can be increased by setting it to only turn on upon motion detection. Average cost - $180AU 

Computer Snooptek Stick	Easy to operate, once this usb stick has been inserted into a target computer, it automatically installs software which will enable that computer to be monitored from another computer anywhere in the world. It can be set to record a range of information such as all keys typed on the keyboard, anything viewed on the screen, both sides of video calls, etc. Average cost - $100AU. 
Recuva software	This software allows you to recover deleted files from your computer or removable devices such as phones, ipods and cameras. A limited version is free to use and can be downloaded from: https://www.piriform.com/recuva 

Sim Card Reader	This device will clone a sim card to obtain all text messages and phone numbers from it, including many which have been deleted by the user. Average cost $10AU 
Hire a Hacker	Computer hackers have become increasingly easy to hire in recent years. Although many operate as 'certified ethical hackers' which have official qualifications for their work and are hired to test security systems permission from the owner, they can easily be hired to crack an email address or Facebook password. Although they often require their clients to agree to a disclaimer that the email address or Facebook account does actually belong to the client, such a measure is not adequate to deter people from hiring them to illegally crack a password or hack into a computer system. Much like ebay, a job can be posted which the prospective hackers then bid on.

	HACKERS LIST
Infidelity detection kit	The 'Checkmate' infidelity kit will detect male and female semen on clothing by blotting paper with a special liquid on it onto clothing. If the paper turns purple, it has detected semen. Average cost - $50AU

5 HIRE A PI

There are several reasons you may wish to consider hiring a licensed private investigator:

1. To perform a more thorough desktop investigation. Licensed private investigators often not only have considerably more experience in this area than yourself, but also have access to subscription databases which contain details such as current address and phone numbers for residential tenants, company directors and property owners;

2. To conduct surveillance. In most countries to follow somebody without their knowledge could be classed as stalking unless they are a licensed private investigator; and

3. To coach you on additional avenues to perform your own investigation.

Surveillance

Once you have profiled your person of interest and have a strong idea of where they are likely to go and who they are likely to meet, you may wish to hire a licensed private investigator to follow them.

Unfortunately, Hollywood has done a terrible job of representing this industry. Although scenes of Magnum PI speeding through the streets in a bright red Ferrari come to mind, this draws little to no resemblance to the reality of performing surveillance.

The following is a general guide to how surveillance would be performed:

- A surveillance vehicle of a bland, common colour such as black, grey or white would be chosen – or a vehicle which will blend into the area such as a 4WD for rural jobs;
- The vehicle will have the darkest legal tint on the windows along with appropriate window shades;
- The vehicle will often be parked towards the end of the street several hundred metres from the target property to reduce the risk of detection;
- The success rate in surveillance will be considerably increased by the use of more than one vehicle and operative;
- Law abiding surveillance operatives will generally not use GPS tracking devices and thus need to rely on other resources which may help to predict where the person of interest may be going such as data provided in the profile you provide, a thorough desktop investigation and a profile built up by surveillance over a period of days/weeks;
- Surveillance operatives carry a range of photographic equipment including camcorders for viewing the person of interest from a distance and a high quality law enforcement grade covert camera such as a Lawmate keyring camera which can be used in a range of light to dark lighted environments such as a nightclub.

CLOSING WORDS

Good luck with your quest to obtain the information you seek. Please do use this information responsibly and if you have any queries or would like a quote on a desktop investigation please feel free to contact me on darrenleeauthor@gmail.com

OTHER BOOKS BY THE AUTHOR

In addition to his career as an insurance defence lawyer and private investigator Darren Lee has worked as a nightclub security professional for over a decade and published his first book *101 Tips on How to Be a Bouncer: Techniques to Handle Situations Without Violence* in 2012. This book was the culmination of many years of personal trial and error by the author in learning the most practical and workable techniques of crowd control in retaining control and gaining compliance using primarily verbal judo and as little physical contact as possible.

The following review was provided by Geoff Thompson - *Author of Dead or Alive: The Choice is Yours* and veteran ex-doorman

"This is a fabulous Book.
I wish I'd had it twenty years ago. How much hassle I could have avoided.
The words are informed, empirical and in places profound.
This is the 'door' bible for a new age.
Highly recommended."

Available now at: http://www.amazon.com/101-Tips-How-Bouncer-Techniques/dp/1479194026

Do-It-Yourself Private Investigations

ABOUT THE AUTHOR

Darren is currently working as a Correctional Officer in an Australian prison. Prior to that he has held a wide range of positions as a nightclub doorman for over a decade, private investigator and an insurance defence lawyer. He has a keen interest in security and investigation training and establishing Open Source Intelligence (Desktop Investigation) systems for private investigation companies. Darren can be contacted at darrenleeauthor@gmail.com

www.ingramcontent.com/pod-product-compliance
Lightning Source LLC
Chambersburg PA
CBHW040325010626
45792CB00024B/2128